You will need:

Rub the butter and plain flour with your fingertips.

Add the cheese and mix it in.

fork

Add a small pinch of mustard, and mix.

a pinch

Crack the egg and whisk it with a fork.

Add the egg to the mix of flour, butter, and cheese.

Mix it until it sticks together and forms a ball. Add some milk if needed.

Wrap the mix and chill it.

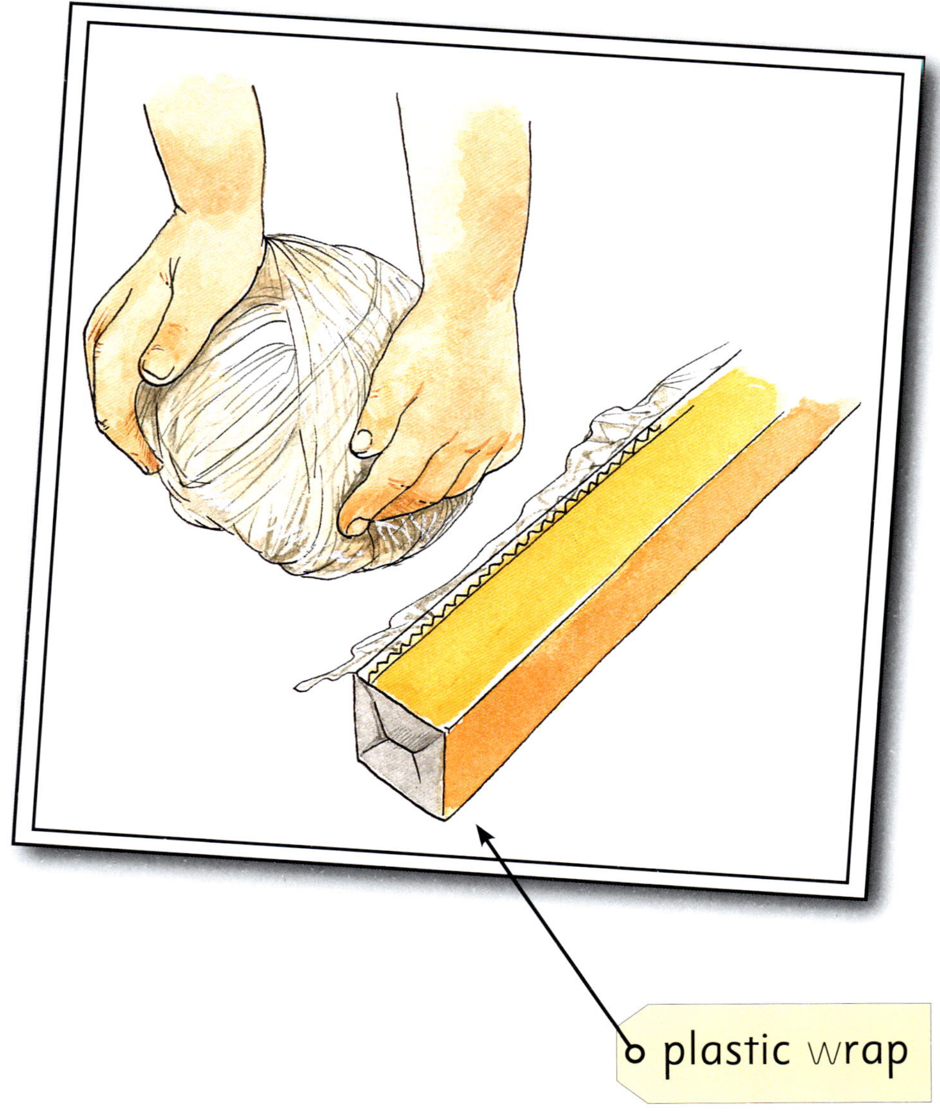

Flatten the mix until it is about as thick as your finger.

Cut out some stars.

Scatter some cheese on top and cook for ten mins, or until you can smell the cheese.

Lift the stars off the sheet and wait for them to cool.

Pack them in a box, as a gift, or...

...munch them, mmmmmm!